42 Guitar Chords Everyone Should Know

A Complete Step-By-Step Guide To
Mastering 42 Of The Most Important Guitar Chords

MICAH BROOKS

WORSHIPHEART

PUBLISHING | EST. 1985

Copyright Information

Resources

Find out about the other books in this series and sign up for the Micah Brooks "Stay Connected" mailing list.

This is book two in the Micah Brooks Guitar Authority Series books. *Worship Guitar In Six Weeks* is a six week course designed to bring a guitar player from knowing little about guitar onto the stage in six weeks. Please pass it along to your friends! Also, the next book in this series is called *Guitar Secrets Revealed*. Learn what the guitar professionals know without needing to spend years to acquire that information. Find out about the Micah Brooks Guitar Authority Series books and more at:

www.micahbrooks.com

Email Micah

Email Micah Brooks at micah@micahbrooks.com. I want to know who you are. I have a heart to meet people. It is my privilege to respond to my emails personally. Please feel free to connect with me. I will glad to answer questions or set up a Skype call as you need.

Join the Micah Brooks "Stay Connected" mailing list to stay up to date

Subscribe to the Micah Brooks Ministry "Stay Connected" mailing list and stay current with my latest book releases. My email list is always free and intended to deliver high value content to your inbox. I do not sell your email address to anyone else. I simply want to be able to stay connected with you. Click here to join my mailing list.

www.micahbrooks.com/join

Reviews on Amazon

Reviews are the lifeblood of authors. If you are willing to leave feedback, I would be humbled and grateful. Please do so at:

www.amazon.com

Skype Lessons

I would be glad to consider giving you online guitar lessons. If you would like to apply for lessons with Micah Brooks via Skype visit my website to find out more. I cannot accept every student, but I would be happy to hear your story and see what you would like to accomplish.

www.micahbrooks.com

Join The Christian Guitar Community Facebook Group

All readers of this book are welcome to join The Christian Guitar Community Facebook group. Meet guitar players from around the world. You may post your insights about learning guitar. You are welcome to ask questions and comment on other posts. The group is designed to be a community. We ask everyone in the group to interact, which makes the content fun and engaging.

www.facebook.com/groups/thechristianguitarcommunity

More About Micah Brooks Ministry

For more about Micah Brooks and my ministry, including books, CDs, mp3s, clothing and art designs, online store, blogs, devotions, speaking and performing dates please go to:

www.micahbrooks.com

Follow Micah Brooks

Everyone is welcome to follow Micah Brooks on these social media platforms:

Facebook: @micahbrookspage
www.facebook.com/micahbrookspage

Twitter: @mchbrks
www.twitter.com/mchbrks

LinkedIn: Micah Brooks
www.linkedin.com/in/micahbrooks

Instagram: @mchbrks
www.instagram.com/mchbrks

If you have trouble connecting to any of these social media accounts, please visit www.micahbrooks.com.

Micah is Editor In Chief at www.worshippublishing.com, www.uprightpassiveincome.com and www.songwritingcreative.com

Worship Publishing is a resource website that includes books, daily devotions, music, podcasts, product reviews and many more recommendations. Use our wealth of staff writers and high quality guest post content to better your walk with the Lord. Visit: www.worshippublishing.com

Upright Passive Income is a company devoted to helping entrepreneurs achieve their vision and dreams. Everyone should have a side business of some kind and earning passive income is an awesome way to do so. Great examples include self-publishing a book, affiliate marketing and video marketing. Visit: www.uprightpassiveincome.com to learn about all of our high quality services.

Songwriting Creative is a website devoted to songwriting in all forms. From beginner writers to the most advanced, we each still have room to grow and expand our skills and craft. www.songwritingcreative.com is intended to be a songwriting community and we do our best to facilitate. Check it out.

Recommendations

Praise for Micah Brooks and
42 Guitar Chords Everyone Should Know

"Micah's new book serves as great inspiration and knowledge for both new and seasoned guitarists. With simple diagrams, he shows how to fret the chord and details the music theory behind the chord construction. If you've ever been intimidated with the process of learning to play guitar or learning how/why chords "earned" their names, 42 Chords takes a simplistic approach to all of it. Not only can it ignite your playing, but it may open up a new world for composition as well. Nicely done!"

-**Chris Wormer** Guitarist for The Charlie Daniels Band

"What a well written book! This composition not only highlights every single chord known to music, it also delivers the information in such a clear and intelligent way. Micah goes on to even show which chords belong together in musical relation, allowing the reader to instantly begin using this information in a creative way. His heart for worship and education is clear from his introductory prayer, the breakdown of each chord and it's level of difficulty, the explanation of how these chords relate to their musical application, to his final blessing for each and every reader. Get this book today!"

-**Doug Carter** Band Leader for Lee Greenwood: Best known for his hit song *God Bless The U.S.A.*

"Micah has hit a home run with this book, very well written yet easy to understand for even the most novice of guitar players. You'll not only learn every chord that can be played on a guitar but it's written in such a clear and easy way you can't help but become a better player. Micah's heart for the reader is easy to see in this book and you'll be glad you bought *42 Guitar Chords Everyone Should Know*…go buy it today!"

-**Gary Miller** Executive Director for www.WorshipMinistry.com

"Whether you are a beginner or have been around the block to this thing called music, this book is a super handy reference. I love that it doesn't just show you the chord, but helps you learn what makes up the chord. In essence, it's the knowledge that takes you from good to great. Now, get those fingers and six strings ready to play some music!"

-**Yancy** Artist, Songwriter and Worship Leader
for Families: www.YancyMinistries.com

"Every guitar player can learn something from this book. There are fundamental ideas that beginners need to know and finer details for more advanced players."

-**Dylan Rosson** Lead Guitarist for
American Idol's Scotty McCreery

"Micah breaks down the anatomy of creating chords on the guitar in an easy-to-understand, do-it-yourself way. The lessons from the book will help diligent students play chord progressions to their favorite songs in no time! I recommend this book to anyone—young, old or in between—who wants to experience the joy of playing guitar."

-**Jamie Harvill** Worship Leader, Teacher, Author and Songwriter:
Ancient Of Days, Because We Believe
and *Garments Of Praise*

"*42 Guitar Chords Everyone Should Know* is just what I and my guitar playing students need. It's foundational, systematic and practical. What's more, it's clear and easy to understand…for anyone. I haven't played for years and love using this book to get back into it. If you want to expand your guitar skills and become a more consistent, predictable guitarist this tool is for you and those you play with."

-**Chris Beatty** President and Founder of www.VocalCoach.com:
Training for singers. He and his wife Carole have sold
over 2 1/2 million training products around the world.

"This book will certainly prove to be a springboard for every learning guitarist, as well as a "must have" in the tool belt of guitarists of all levels. Micah has effectively mapped out what should be the foundation of all musicians desiring to gain a well-rounded knowledge of the guitar."

-Ben Radliff Worship Pastor for
Christ Community Church in St. Charles, IL

"This is an excellent resource for every guitar player. It is easy to follow and is laid out in a very helpful way for both beginner guitarists and more experienced ones. As a worship leader who uses piano as my primary instrument, I found this book incredibly helpful to understand more about the guitar and I plan to buy this book for the guitarists on my worship team."

-Kevin Kruse Worship Pastor for
Laurelwood Baptist Church in Vancouver, WA
and Co-Host of www.WorshipMinistryCatalyst.com Podcast

"This book is a great resource for any guitarist! Micah's passion for teaching is evident in this easy to read book that goes beyond the typical chord book. His straightforward explanation of guitar theory is very insightful without getting overly complicated and loosing the reader. The easy layout makes it perfect to use for quick reference. I would highly recommend this book to anyone looking to sharpen their guitar skills!"

-Ben Davis Worship Arts Pastor for
First Baptist Church in Clarksville, TN

Dedication

A very special thank you to my wife, Rochelle, and my children Liam, Aisley and Jovie. Without you this would not have been possible. You have my deepest love and affection. I continue to dedicate my books to you!

Table Of Contents

Worship Guitar In Six Weeks

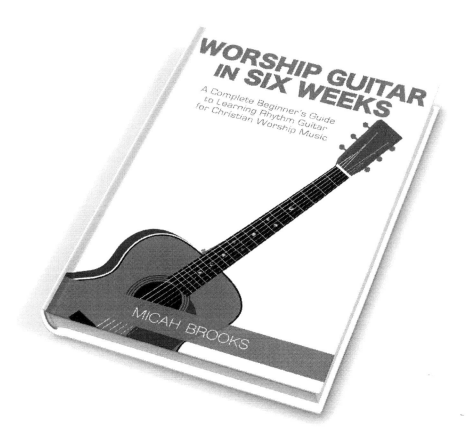

42 Guitar Chords Everyone Should Know is the second in the Micah Brooks guitar book series. If you are new to learning guitar, I strongly recommend you check out *Worship Guitar In Six Weeks* first. Then come back to this book. You will learn all the fundamentals of guitar you need when learning guitar chords. Plus, there are recommendations for how to change your strings, use a metronome and how to tune. The book is a six week course for a new guitar player to begin with little guitar knowledge and then be able to play with a worship team by the end of the six week course. This course is proven to work! Over one thousand people have given it a try! Pick up *Worship Guitar In Six Weeks* today.

Guitar Secrets Revealed

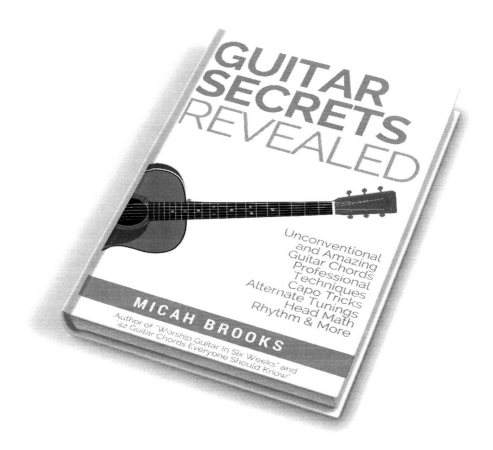

This is the book that I wish every professional guitarist would write. I would buy their book and they buy mine. These are the tricks and shortcuts that I have learned over fifteen years of playing guitar professionally. In *Guitar Secrets Revealed* I present unconventional and less traditional, but better ways to play fundamental chords. Inside are methods of using the thumb to play chords that you never knew existed. Learn all about "head math" which is really practical music theory ready for the stage. This is not boring college music theory lectures, rather the most boots-on-the-ground way to understand numbers and how to use them to memorize any song quickly and easily. I also demonstrate some awesome ways to use your capo and alternate tunings for your guitar. This is just the beginning of what is in this book. Get your copy today.

- - - - -

Introduction

Welcome to *42 Guitar Chords Everyone Should Know*! Thank you for purchasing this book! I appreciate that you are willing to use my teaching experience to better your guitar skills. I recognize this as a privilege and consider it my honor!

Most apparent from the title of this book is that by the time you finish you will have learned 42 guitar chords. What is not as easy to see is the method you will use for learning each one. Each chapter teaches an individual guitar chord. This is so you can skip around later if you would like. My recommendation on the front end is that you go on the journey as it is laid out. This book is planned much like how you can walk the aisles of an IKEA store. You can either walk the short cut routes and miss something or take the long, planned out route and see everything. Each chord has an intentional link to the next one. You may place your finger on a certain fret in the first chord and leave it there for the second. This helps in transitioning. That said, every chord stands alone. You may jump around as you wish!

Let's Pray!

Before we dive in, I always begin any of my guitar lessons with prayer. The reason is simple but important. With all my heart I believe that God created music. He created music for the purpose of allowing us to minister to Him and to be creative before Him. David demonstrated this hundreds of times in the Old Testament. Thank you for allowing me to pray over you.

"Lord Jesus, I thank You for this precious guitarist. I pray that as they are diligent in learning this craft, You would add to their learning. May You ignite in them a passion for Your name and a desire to please You through music. Please work in them as they use their new ability to glorify You and extend Your kingdom. In Jesus' name, amen."

A note about how to use each chord

Every chord has a **chord name**, **diagram**, **chord information section** and a step-by-step **finger position section**. Here is how to use each one:

A. Chord Name

Your first inclination may be to move past the **chord name** and right into learning the chord itself. I recommend spending time learning each chord's name. Besides being what the chord is known as, it gives you characteristics about the chord you need to know. First, you will see the fundamental (or root) note. This is the first letter or series of letters in the name. For example, in a "DMaj7" the "D" is the fundamental note being played. The last piece of the name is the chord suffix. The chord suffix is the series of letters that follow the fundamental note. This is known as the tone modifier of the chord. In this book you will see these modifiers: "Major", "Minor", "sus", "2", "add9", "Maj7", "7", "m7" and "6".

Major Chords

Major chords are built on the 1, 3, 5 tones of the major scale. They are the fundamental chords from which all other chords derive. You will learn 12 major chords in this book. We will use the "C" chord as a practical example in each of these chord name sections. In a "C" major chord, the notes are "C", "E" and "G". The "C" scale has no flat or sharp notes in it. There are only natural notes, or white keys if you are familiar with a piano. As we move along we will add to or modify this "C" chord.

Please note, the explanation above assumes you are speaking about the tonic or root chord of any key. A more formal way of describing a major chord is to say that all major chords have three semitones between the low note and the middle note and two semitones between the middle note and the higher note. This description may be a little too complex for beginners. Continue on and as you learn each chord you may begin to recognize music theory related patterns that will make this clearer.

Minor Chords

Minor chords are built as the 1, ♭3, 5 tones of the scale. From a major chord, you flatten the third note in the scale (♭3) to create a minor chord. These chords are fundamentally different, but may look similar on paper. You may notice that major chords tend to sound "bright" while minor chords "dark" in nature. For our "C" chord example, the notes are "C", "E♭" and "G". Notice the same first and fifth notes in the scale, but the third note has been flattened. This changes the property of the chord, making it "minor".

"sus" Chords

"sus" chords, or "suspended" chords, are built as 1, 4, 5 tones in a scale. You omit the third tone in the scale and replace it with the fourth. This modifies the chord to have a *suspended in the air* type sound. To the ear, the fourth note suspends and then wants to revert back to the third note that has been removed. This may be confusing at this point, but when you build these chords you will understand the interaction. Building on our "C" chord example, our notes are "C", "F" and "G". The "E" note has been removed replacing it with the "F", which creates the suspension.

"2" and "add9" Chords

"2" and **"add9" chords** are essentially the same chord but with different names. The "2" chord adds the second note in the scale (either keeping the third note or omitting it, both are possible). The "add9" chord adds a ninth note to the scale. A major scale is only eight notes, so the ninth note is the second note of the scale after it repeats moving upward musically. Here is how to build these two chords. To build the "2" chord, it is 1, 2, 3 (optional) and 5. To build the "add9" chord, it is 1, 3, 5, 8 (which is just the repeat of 1, but up eight notes, or an octave) and 9 (which is the 2 note, but up an octave, making it a 9 note). Let's use our "C" example for both chords. In a "2" chord for "C" you have a "C", "D", "E" (optional) and "G". For the "add9" it is "C", "E", "G", "C" (optional) and the "D". You can see that both chords are built using the same notes. The difference is where those notes live in the chord. If this is confusing you should be able to hear the differences as you learn in this book. One last note, in most cases you will encounter "2" chords over "add9". We learned the "add9" chord only because the "Cadd9" chord is a very popular guitar chord.

"Maj7" Chords

"Maj7" chords are built exactly as a major chord, except you add the major seventh note of the scale to the chord. The chord would be built as 1, 3, 5, 7. It is important to note that this is the 7 of the scale and not the ♭7 of the scale. You will hear the difference as you build "Maj7" and "7" chords. To continue our "C" chord example, the notes are: "C", "E", "G" and "B". "Maj7" chords tend to sound melancholy.

"7" Chords

"7" chords assume a flattened seventh note in the major scale. This is an established rule in music theory. The chord is built: 1, 3, 5, ♭7. Typically, the added flat seventh note creates a twangy characteristic to the chord. It is easy to confuse "Maj7" and "7" chords. They share similar names, but as you will found out, they sound completely different. As far as our "C" chord it would be a "C", "E", "G" and "B♭".

"m7" Chords

"m7" chords, like "7" chords, assume a flattened seventh note in the major scale. The "m7" builds from the minor chord discussed above. As a side note, this ♭7 note of the major scale is the *regular* seventh note in the minor scale. A minor scale is 1, 2, ♭3, 4, 5, ♭6, ♭7 and then 8 (or 1 repeated). To build the "m7" chord we use 1, ♭3, 5, ♭7. For a "Cm7" the notes would be "C", "E♭", "G" and "B♭".

"6" Chords

"6" chords add the sixth note of the major scale to a major chord. A "6" chord would be 1, 3, 5 and 6. Depending on how you build the chord, you may or may not include the fifth note in the scale. Both are correct. The option is there because the 5 and the 6 are so close to each other in tone that they can sound dissonant, or unresolved. This is especially true when those notes are played lower musically. In our "C" example this would be built: "C", "E", "G" and "A".

B. Chord Diagram

Every chord has a unique **chord diagram**. There are several parts in each one. In this section they are explained. Refer back to this diagram as you begin learning.

Chord Diagram Explained

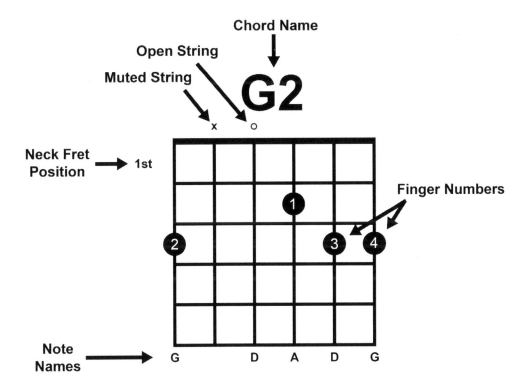

Chord Name

This section is to describe the name of the chord. This may include a chord suffix, like "C6" where the "6" is the modifier.

Open String

An open string is a guitar string that is played with no finger touching it. The note name is the string's name. For example, if you play an open fourth string (like in this "G2" chord example), the open note being played on the [D] string is a "D".

Muted String

A muted string is one that is either being muted by a neighboring finger or intentionally not being played with the right, strumming hand. In this example of the "G2" chord, the fifth string [A] is not being played.

Neck Fret Position

The neck fret position number is important to always notice when reviewing a chord diagram. That number signifies the starting position of your fingers on the neck. It can go as high as the last fret on your guitar. If you see a "1st" denotation then the chord is played in open position at the beginning of the neck. "1st" is the *home base* position on the guitar. Everything else is related to that home base position. Were you to see "3rd", like in a "C#" chord, then your root note begins on the fourth fret. Do your best to observe the neck fret position indication for each chord.

Finger Numbers

While you could use nicknames for each finger on your left hand (like pointer finger, pinky, etc.) most guitar teachers will use numbers for each finger. Using numbers allows for quick reference as you get into chord diagrams and transitioning.

Here is how I detail each finger of the left hand. The pointer finger (index finger) is (1). Your middle finger is (2), ring finger is (3) and pinky finger (4). I label the thumb (T). While you will not get into any thumb playing in this book, you may as you improve in your skills moving on to further chording. Note: left handed guitarists will use the opposite hand, making each of the labels above true for the *right hand* rather than the left.

Note Names

Below each chord diagram are the note names being played per string. Please notice that these are not the root names of the strings when being played open. Rather, these are the notes being played after fretting the chord. Some of the notes will be the open notes, but only when there is no finger needed for that particular string in the chord. When a string is being omitted or muted, no note name will be present.

C. Chord Information

Each chord has a section called **chord information**. These sections are made to be quick glance reference points for you as you begin to master your chords. Here is each part of the "Chord Information" section explained:

"G2" Chord Information:
- Number of Strings Used: Five (5)
- Level of Difficulty: Moderate
- Related Chords: G, Dsus, Em7

Number Of Strings Used

This is a quick glance reference of the **number of strings used** when you finish fretting your chord. If the number "six" is used then you strum every string. If any less than six, like "five" as in the example above, then at least one string has been omitted. Note that the number of strings being omitted is not always the bottom strings. They can be muted middle strings. In our "G2" example, the fifth string [A] is being muted, thus in this chord you only strum five strings. This chord is unique in that you technically strum across all six strings, however you are muting that fifth string [A].

Level Of Difficulty

The **level of difficulty** is an opinion of how hard this chord is compared to others in this book. The level of difficulty assumes that you haven't learned any of these chords before. In many cases, students are beginning with some prior guitar knowledge. Please only use the "Level Of Difficulty" as my opinion.

Related Chords

Related chords are ones that play well with the chord you are learning. These are by no means the only chords that are related. Rather, these are to get you started. You will learn several other related chords by the end of this manual. If you find a related chord you do not know yet, be patient. You will get there. I suppose you could skip ahead if you wanted.

D. Finger Position Section

From my experience, what sets this book apart from other teaching manuals is the **finger position section**. A great guitar instructor does not just show his/her student a chord diagram. He or she will take you through a step-by-step process that explains to you the most efficient and beneficial way to play a chord. The methods presented here are the *tried and true*. That being noted, you can place your fingers into the chord positions however you would like.

Use the "Finger Position Section" as your personal guitar coach walking you through each chord's steps. There are recommendations for how to transition to other chords. There are also tricks that I have learned over years of experience that you can employ after you have completed the step by step process.

A few last ideas before we begin

In every case where an open chord could be used, this book teaches it. An open chord is one where each finger only plays one note and does not barre across multiple strings. There is usually at least one open string in an open chord. These tend to be easier to play and they often sound richer. Barre chords are only used when necessary and when an open chord alternative is not available. All of the open chords in this book can be played as barre chords; however, it would be more difficult to do so.

A barre chord is a way of fretting a chord by holding down multiple strings with a single finger. In many cases your index finger (1) will be laid across several strings to create barre chords.

#'s vs. ♭'s

One final word before we begin, the terms sharp (#) and flat (♭) are essentially the same thing. These are literally two names for the same note. I chose to write all the chords as sharps (#'s) in this book with the flattened (♭) counterpart written in a lighter shade beside it because guitar players tend to play #'s. However, you need to take time to learn both names for each # and ♭ chord.

Before You Begin

I am available to all of my readers. I want to hear from you. If you have any questions, comments or feedback, please email me at micah@micahbrooks.com. I look forward to responding.

It is time to begin your 42 guitar chord journey!

— — — — —

Main Major Chords

— — — — —

"G"

"D"

"C"

"A"

"E"

In this section you will learn several major chords. Here is a review of what a major chord is.

Major Chords

Major chords are built on the 1, 3, 5 tones of the major scale. They are the fundamental chords from which all other chords derive. You will learn 12 major chords in this book. We will use the "C" chord as a practical example in each of these chord name sections. In a "C" major chord, the notes are "C", "E" and "G". The "C" scale has no flat or sharp notes in it. There are only natural notes, or white keys if you are familiar with a piano. As we move along we will add to or modify this "C" chord.

Please note, the explanation above assumes you are speaking about the tonic or root chord of any key. A more formal way of describing a major chord is to say that all major chords have three semitones between the low note and the middle note and two semitones between the middle note and the higher note. This description may be a little too complex for beginners. Continue on and as you learn each chord you may begin to recognize music theory related patterns that will make this clearer.

"G" Chord

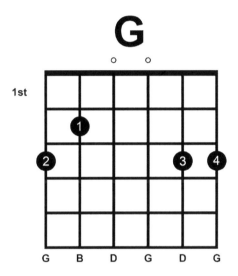

"G" Chord Information:

- Number of Strings Used: Six (6)
- Level of Difficulty: Easy
- Related Chords: Cadd9, Dsus, Em7

Follow this fingering progression to play a "G" chord:

Place your pointer finger (1) on the second fret of the fifth string [A]. Follow with your middle finger (2) on the third fret of the sixth string [E]. Last, add your ring (3) and pinky fingers (4) to the third frets of both the second [B] and first [e] strings, respectively. Those final fingers should be tight fitting. Strum across all six strings and you will have a "G" chord. This is a fundamental guitar chord and will relate to many others throughout this book.

"D" Chord

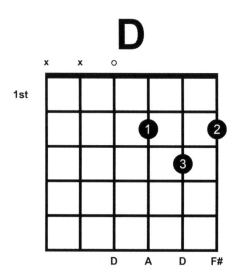

"D" Chord Information:

- Number of Strings Used: Four (4)
- Level of Difficulty: Easy
- Related Chords: G, Cadd9, Em7

Follow this fingering progression to play a "D" chord:

Begin by placing your pointer finger (1) on the second fret of the third string [G]. Add your middle finger (2) to the second fret of the first string [e]. Last, add your ring finger (3) to the third fret of the second string [B]. Strum the bottom four strings and you are playing "D". Make sure you omit the low [E] and [A] strings when you strum this chord.

"C" Chord

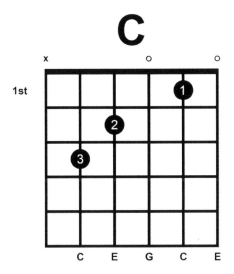

"C" Chord Information:

- Number of Strings Used: Five (5)
- Level of Difficulty: Easy
- Related Chords: G, Em, Am

Follow this fingering progression to play a "C" chord:

Begin by placing the index finger (1) on the first fret of the second string [B]. Make sure you make excellent contact with that string without muting the third [G] and first [e] strings around it. Strum those top three strings to confirm you have proper positioning. Next, add your middle finger (2) to the second fret of the fourth string [D], again making great contact. Finally, add your ringer finger (3) to the third fret of the fifth string [A]. Strum this chord across the last five strings, muting or not strumming the sixth string [E].

"A" Chord

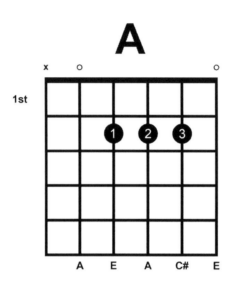

"A" Chord Information:

- Number of Strings Used: Five (5)
- Level of Difficulty: Easy
- Related Chords: E, D, G

Follow this fingering progression to play an "A" chord:

There are multiple fingerings for the standard "A" chord. I am going to demonstrate the main version; however, future books or the internet may show you others. Begin by placing your index finger (1) onto the second fret of the fourth string [D]. Continue by placing your middle finger (2) onto the second fret of the third string [G]. Last, place your ring finger (3) on the second fret of the second string [B]. Strum the last five strings, omitting the low [E] string. You need to practice getting into this position often, as muscle memory will develop.

"E" Chord

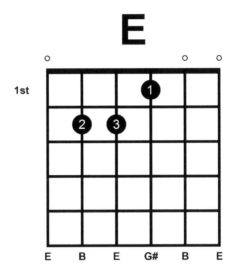

"E" Chord Information:

- Number of Strings Used: Six (6)
- Level of Difficulty: Easy
- Related Chords: A, D, B

Follow this fingering progression to play an "E" chord:

Begin by placing your middle finger (2) on the second fret of the fifth string [A]. Next set your ring finger (3) onto the second fret of the fourth string [D]. Finally, and this takes some stretching, place your index finger (1) onto the first fret of the third string [G]. Strum all six strings. At first, you may have a tendency to let up on the third string. Doing so changes the tone of the chord. Make sure you can hear each individual string and note clearly.

Main Minor Chords

"Em"
"Dm"
"Am"

In this section you will learn minor chords. Here is a review of minor chords.

Minor Chords

Minor chords are built as the 1, ♭3, 5 tones of the scale. From a major chord, you flatten the third note in the scale (♭3) to create a minor chord. These chords are fundamentally different, but may look similar on paper. You may notice that major chords tend to sound "bright" while minor chords "dark" in nature. For our "C" chord example, the notes are "C", "E♭" and "G". Notice the same first and fifth notes in the scale, but the third note has been flattened. This changes the property of the chord, making it "minor".

"Em" Chord

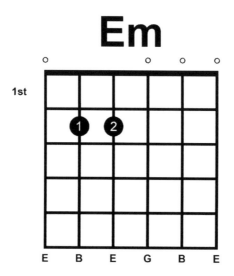

"Em" Chord Information:

- Number of Strings Used: Six (6)
- Level of Difficulty: Easy
- Related Chords: G, D, C

Follow this fingering progression to play an "Em" chord:

Place your pointer finger (1) onto the second fret of the fifth string [A]. Next, and finally, as this chord is easy to fret, add your middle finger (2) to the second fret of the fourth string [D]. Strum all six strings to play "Em".

"Dm" Chord

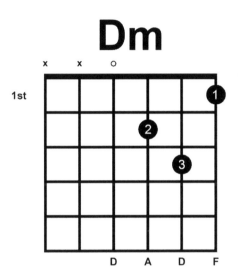

"Dm" Chord Information:

- Number of Strings Used: Four (4)
- Level of Difficulty: Easy
- Related Chords: F, C, G

Follow this fingering progression to play a "Dm" chord:

Start by placing your middle finger (2) on the second fret of the third [G] string. Add the ring finger (3) to the third fret of the second [B] string. Finally, put your index finger (1) onto the first fret of the first [e] string. Once in place, strum the last four strings. The top note that your index finger (1) is playing is the note that makes the chord a *minor*. Make sure that you hear that note when you strum all four strings.

"Am" Chord

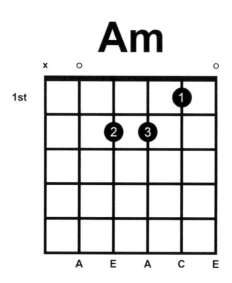

"Am" Chord Information:
- Number of Strings Used: Five (5)
- Level of Difficulty: Easy
- Related Chords: C, Em, G

Follow this fingering progression to play an "Am" chord:

Start by placing the index finger (1) on the first fret of the second string [B]. Then add your middle finger (2) to the second fret of the fourth string [D]. Last, add your ring finger (3) to the second fret of the third string [G]. You may be noticing the tight squeeze of all three fingers quite close together. This is normal. With good upright pressure with your left hand, all three fingers will fit into their proper place. Strum only the bottom five strings.

— — — — —

Major Chord Modifiers

— — — — —

"Dsus"
"D2"
"Asus"
"A2"
"A7"
"Esus"

In this section you will learn "sus", "2" and "7" chords. Here is a review of each type of chord.

"sus" Chords

"sus" chords, or "suspended" chords, are built as 1, 4, 5 tones in a scale. You omit the third tone in the scale and replace it with the fourth. This modifies the chord to have a *suspended in the air* type sound. To the ear, the fourth note suspends and then wants to revert back to the third note that has been removed. This may be confusing at this point, but when you build these chords you will understand the interaction. Building on our "C" chord

41

example, our notes are "C", "F" and "G". The "E" note has been removed replacing it with the "F", which creates the suspension.

"2" and "add9" Chords

"2" and **"add9" chords** are essentially the same chord but with different names. The "2" chord adds the second note in the scale (either keeping the third note or omitting it, both are possible). The "add9" chord adds a ninth note to the scale. A major scale is only eight notes, so the ninth note is the second note of the scale after it repeats moving upward musically. Here is how to build these two chords. To build the "2" chord, it is 1, 2, 3 (optional) and 5. To build the "add9" chord, it is 1, 3, 5, 8 (which is just the repeat of 1, but up eight notes, or an octave) and 9 (which is the 2 note, but up an octave, making it a 9 note). Let's use our "C" example for both chords. In a "2" chord for "C" you have a "C", "D", "E" (optional) and "G". For the "add9" it is "C", "E", "G", "C" (optional) and the "D". You can see that both chords are built using the same notes. The difference is where those notes live in the chord. If this is confusing you should be able to hear the differences as you learn in this book. One last note, in most cases you will encounter "2" chords over "add9". We learned the "add9" chord only because the "Cadd9" chord is a very popular guitar chord.

"7" Chords

"7" chords assume a flattened seventh note in the major scale. This is an established rule in music theory. The chord is built: 1, 3, 5, $\flat$7. Typically, the added flat seventh note creates a twangy characteristic to the chord. It is easy to confuse "Maj7" and "7" chords. The share similar names, but as you will found out, they sound completely different. As far as our "C" chord it would be a "C", "E", "G" and "B$\flat$".

"Dsus" Chord

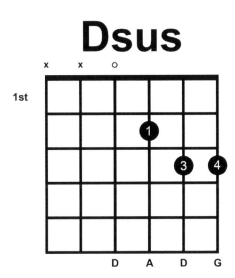

"Dsus" Chord Information:

- Number of Strings Used: Four (4)
- Level of Difficulty: Easy
- Related Chords: D, G, Cadd9

Follow this fingering progression to play a "Dsus" chord:

The best place to begin with a "Dsus" is by placing your index finger (1) on the second fret of the third string [G]. Then add your ring finger (3) to the third fret of the second string [B]. The final step is to add your pinky finger (4) to the third fret of the first string [e]. Strum the last four strings. Note that this chord transitions quickly to the "D" chord. You only need to take off your pinky finger (4) from the first string [e] replacing it with your middle finger (2)

43

on the second fret of the same first string [e]. Then you will have transitioned to the "D" chord from "Dsus". Practice this transition. You will use it often as you progress on the guitar.

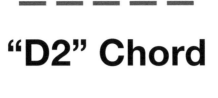

"D2" Chord

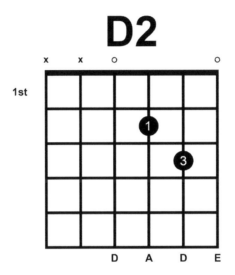

"D2" Chord Information:

- Number of Strings Used: Four (4)
- Level of Difficulty: Easy
- Related Chords: G, D, Em7

Follow this fingering progression to play a "D2" chord:

The first of two steps is to place your index finger (1) onto the second fret of the third string [G]. Last, add your ring finger (3) to the third fret of the second string [B]. Strum the last four strings. Notice that you can begin with a "D" chord and remove your middle finger (2) from the second fret of the first string [e] to transition to a "D2". Practice this transition. As well, practice playing "D" to "Dsus" and then to "D2". Each of those are commonly related chords that you will find out in the wild as you play guitar.

"Asus" Chord

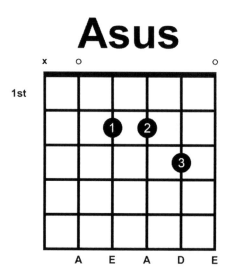

"Asus" Chord Information:

- Number of Strings Used: Five (5)
- Level of Difficulty: Easy
- Related Chords: A, G, D

Follow this fingering progression to play an "Asus" chord:

Begin by placing your pointer finger (1) onto the second fret of the fourth string [D]. Next, add your middle finger (2) on the second fret of the third string [G]. The final step is to place your ring finger (3) on the third fret of the second [B] string. Those fingers should fit tightly together. Strum only the last five strings. This chord transitions well to it's closest cousin, the "A" chord.

"A2" Chord

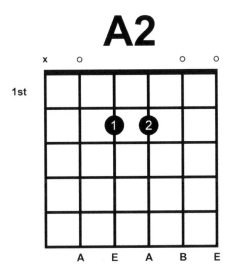

"A2" Chord Information:

- Number of Strings Used: Five (5)
- Level of Difficulty: Easy
- Related Chords: E, D, F#m7

Follow this fingering progression to play an "A2" chord:

Place your pointer finger (1) on the second fret of the fourth string [D]. Follow that with your middle finger (2) on the second fret of the third string [G]. Those fingers should fit tightly together. Strum only the last 5 strings.

"A7" Chord

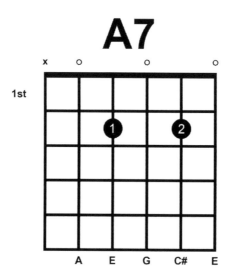

"A7" Chord Information:

- Number of Strings Used: Five (5)
- Level of Difficulty: Easy
- Related Chords: E7, D, G

Follow this fingering progression to play an "A7" chord:

Start by placing your index finger (1) onto the second fret of the fourth string [D]. The only other finger to use in this chord is your middle finger (2) on the second fret of the second string [B]. Strum the last five strings, omitting the low [E] string. Notice that the third string [G] is open and not being touched by any fingers. This needs to be true to create the "7" in the "A7". This may sound rather *twangy*.

"Esus" Chord

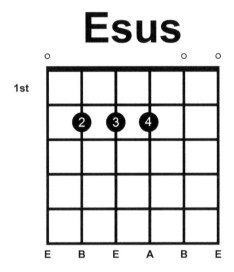

"Esus" Chord Information:

• Number of Strings Used: Six (6)
• Level of Difficulty: Easy
• Related Chords: E, A, D

Follow this fingering progression to play an "Esus" chord:

Begin by placing your middle finger (2) on the second fret of the fifth string [A]. Next, set your ring finger (3) onto the second fret of the fourth string [D]. Last, place your pinky finger (4) onto the second fret of the third string [G]. Strum all six strings. If you will fret an "E" chord before you create this "Esus" you can simply add the pinky finger (4) to the second fret of the third string [G] to create an "Esus". That makes for a great transition between "E" and "Esus".

— — — — — —

"m7" Chords

— — — — — —

"Em7"
"Am7"

In this section you will learn "m7" chords. Here is a review of how to understand "m7" chords.

"m7" Chords

"m7" chords, like "7" chords, assume a flattened seventh note in the major scale. The "m7" builds from the minor chord discussed above. As a side note, this ♭7 note of the major scale is the *regular* seventh note in the minor scale. A minor scale is 1, 2, ♭3, 4, 5, ♭6, ♭7 and then 8 (or 1 repeated). To build the "m7" chord we use 1, ♭3, 5, ♭7. For a "Cm7" the notes would be "C", "E♭", "G" and "B♭".

"Em7" Chord

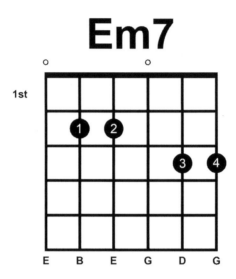

"Em7" Chord Information:

- Number of Strings Used: Six (6)
- Level of Difficulty: Easy
- Related Chords: G, D, C

Follow this fingering progression to play an "Em7" chord:

You begin by placing your index finger (1) and your middle finger (2) onto the second frets of the fifth [A] and fourth [D] strings respectively. This is the same as your "Em" chord learned earlier. Next, add your ring finger (3) and pinky finger (4) to the third frets of the second [B] and first [e] strings, respectively. Strum all six strings. Notice that the notes being played on the third frets of the second [B] and first [e] strings are shared with many chords, including "G", "Cadd9" and "Dsus". This makes for very smoothing transitioning.

"Am7" Chord

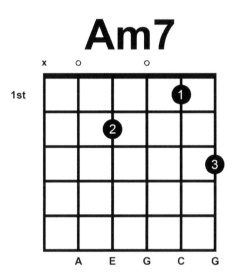

"Am7" Chord Information:
- Number of Strings Used: Five (5)
- Level of Difficulty: Easy
- Related Chords: C, D, G

Follow this fingering progression to play an "Am7" chord:

First, place your index finger (1) on the first fret of the second string [B]. Then add your middle finger (2) to the second fret of the fourth string [D]. Last, add your ring finger (3) to the third fret of the first string [e]. Adding the third finger may be a stretch for you. Do your best to practice this chord often and you will get better at making that stretch. Strum only the last five strings.

▬ ▬ ▬ ▬ ▬

"Maj7" Chords

▬ ▬ ▬ ▬ ▬

"AMaj7"
"CMaj7"
"DMaj7"
"FMaj7"
"GMaj7"

In this section you will learn "Maj7" chords. Here is a review of "Maj7" chords.

"Maj7" Chords

"Maj7" chords are built exactly as a major chord, except you add the major seventh note of the scale to the chord. The chord would be built as 1, 3, 5, 7. It is important to note that this is the 7 of the scale and not the ♭7 of the scale. You will hear the difference as you build "Maj7" and "7" chords. To continue our "C" chord example, the notes are: "C", "E", "G" and "B". "Maj7" chords tend to sound melancholy.

"AMaj7" Chord

AMaj7

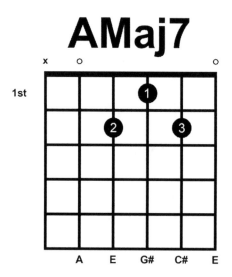

"AMaj7" Chord Information:

- Number of Strings Used: Five (5)
- Level of Difficulty: Moderate
- Related Chords: E, D, F#m

Follow this fingering progression to play an "AMaj7" chord:

Begin by placing your middle finger (2) on the second fret of the fourth string [D]. Next, add your index finger (1) to the first fret of the third string [G]. The final step is to place your ring finger (3) on the second fret of the second string [B]. Note that your fingers will be in a tight package. Strum only the last five strings. This chord may sound rather melancholy to you. That is a characteristic of "Maj7" chords.

56

"CMaj7" Chord

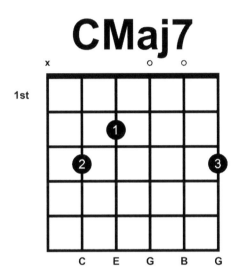

"CMaj7" Chord Information:

- Number of Strings Used: Five (5)
- Level of Difficulty: Easy
- Related Chords: C, G, Em

Follow this fingering progression to play a "CMaj7" chord:

First, add your middle finger (2) onto the third fret of the fifth string [A]. Then add your index finger (1) to the second fret of the fourth string [D]. Last, add your ring finger (3) to the third fret of the first [e] string. Strum the last five strings, always omitting the sixth string [E]. The open note on the second string [B] is what causes the "Maj7" sound in this chord. Confirm you can hear this note in your chord. It is important! Also, you can leave the first string [e] open instead of placing your ring finger (3) onto the third fret. Both are versions of the "CMaj7" chord.

"DMaj7" Chord

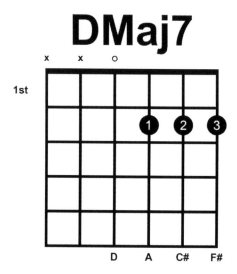

"DMaj7" Chord Information:

- Number of Strings Used: Four (4)
- Level of Difficulty: Easy
- Related Chords: D, A, F#m

Follow this fingering progression to play a "DMaj7" chord:

Start by placing your pointer finger (1) on the second fret of the third string [G]. Next, add your middle finger (2) to the second fret of the second string [B]. Last, place your ring finger (3) onto the second fret of the first string [e]. Strum only the last four strings. The key to playing this chord correctly is by getting all three fingers to form as tight of package as possible. Note that "Esus", "A" and "DMaj7" are all chords formed by placing three fingers on the second fret tightly together.

"FMaj7" Chord

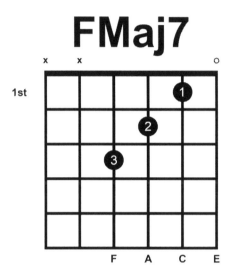

"FMaj7" Chord Information:

- Number of Strings Used: Four (4)
- Level of Difficulty: Easy
- Related Chords: C, Dm, Am

Follow this fingering progression to play a "FMaj7" chord:

Begin by placing your index finger (1) onto the first fret of the second string [B]. Next, add your middle finger (2) to the second fret of the third string [G]. Last, add your ring finger (3) onto the third fret of the fourth string [D]. Strum the last four strings. Make sure to keep the first string [e] open. That "e" note makes the chord a "Maj7".

"GMaj7" Chord

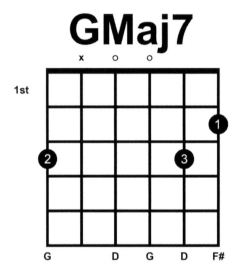

"GMaj7" Chord Information:

- Number of Strings Used: Five (5)
- Level of Difficulty: Hard
- Related Chords: G, D, Em7

Follow this fingering progression to play a "GMaj7" chord:

Place your middle finger (2) onto the third fret of the sixth string [E]. Next, add your ring finger (3) to the third fret of the second string [B]. Finally, stretch your index finger (1) across the fret board to the second fret of the first string [e]. As in other chords, use your middle finger (2) to mute the fifth string [A] by lightly laying it on that string while keeping a tight hold of the third fret of the sixth string [E]. Strum all six strings, though you will be muting the fifth string [A]. Make sure that you hear the first string [e] ringing out. That is the "Maj7" note of "GMaj7". This chord is difficult. The only way to master it is through practice.

"2" and "add9" Chords

"Cadd9"
"F2"
"G2"

In this section you will learn "2" and "add9" chords. Here is a review of "2" and "add9" chords.

"2" and "add9" Chords

"2" and **"add9" chords** are essentially the same chord but with different names. The "2" chord adds the second note in the scale (either keeping the third note or omitting it, both are possible). The "add9" chord adds a ninth note to the scale. A major scale is only eight notes, so the ninth note is the second note of the scale after it repeats moving upward musically. Here is how to build these two chords. To build the "2" chord, it is 1, 2, 3 (optional) and 5. To build the "add9" chord, it is 1, 3, 5, 8 (which is just the repeat of 1, but up eight notes, or an octave) and 9 (which is the 2 note, but up an octave, making it a 9 note). Let's use our "C" example for both chords. In a "2" chord for "C" you have a "C", "D", "E" (optional) and "G". For the "add9" it is "C", "E", "G", "C" (optional) and the "D". You can see that both chords are built using the same notes. The difference is where those notes live in the chord. If this is confusing you should be able to hear the differences as you learn in this book. One last note, in most cases you will encounter "2" chords over "add9". We learned the "add9" chord only because the "Cadd9" chord is a very popular guitar chord.

"Cadd9" Chord

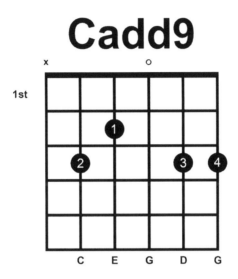

"Cadd9" Chord Information:

- Number of Strings Used: Five (5)
- Level of Difficulty: Easy
- Related Chords: G, Em7, Dsus

Follow this fingering progression to play a "Cadd9" chord:

To begin, place your index finger (1) onto the second fret of the fourth string [D]. Next, add your middle finger (2) to the third fret of the fifth string [A]. Continue by placing your ring (3) and pinky (4) fingers on the third frets of the second [B] and first [e] strings, respectively. Strum only the last five strings, omitting the sixth string [E]. This chord looks similar to the "G" chord and is related.

65

"F2" Chord

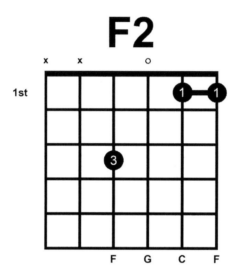

"F2" Chord Information:

- Number of Strings Used: Four (4)
- Level of Difficulty: Moderate
- Related Chords: F, C, Dm

Follow this fingering progression to play a "F2" chord:

First, begin by placing your pointer finger (1) barred across both first frets of the second [B] and the first [e] strings. This barre should be as strong as possible. Make sure you can hear both notes clearly when played individually. Last, add your ring finger (3) on the third fret of the fourth string [D]. Only strum the last four strings, making sure to omit the sixth [E] and fifth [A] strings. Also, make sure that the third string [G] is left open and can be heard when you strum the "F2".

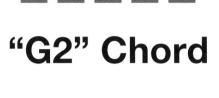

"G2" Chord

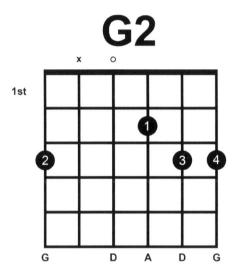

"G2" Chord Information:

- Number of Strings Used: Five (5)
- Level of Difficulty: Moderate
- Related Chords: G, Dsus, Em7

Follow this fingering progression to play a "G2" chord:

Place your pointer finger (1) on the second fret of the third string [G]. Next, add your middle finger (2) on the third fret of the sixth string [E]. Last, add your ring (3) and pinky fingers (4) to the third frets of both the second [B] and first [e] strings, respectively. Those fingers should fit tight together. Your middle finger (2) should lightly touch the fifth string [A] to mute it. This is important. Strum all six strings, omitting the fifth string [A], to form the "G2".

"6" Chords

"G6"
"C6"

In this section you will learn "6" chords. Here is a review of "6" chords.

"6" Chords

"6" chords add the sixth note of the major scale to a major chord. A "6" chord would be 1, 3, 5 and 6. Depending on how you build the chord, you may or may not include the fifth note in the scale. Both are correct. The option is there because the 5 and the 6 are so close to each other in tone that they can sound dissonant, or unresolved. This is especially true when those notes are played lower musically. In our "C" example this would be built: "C", "E", "G" and "A".

"G6" Chord

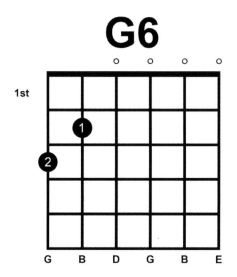

"G6" Chord Information:
- Number of Strings Used: Six (6)
- Level of Difficulty: Easy
- Related Chords: G, D, Em

Follow this fingering progression to play a "G6" chord:

Begin by placing your pointer finger (1) on the second fret of the fifth string [A]. Last, add your middle finger (2) on the third fret of the sixth string [E]. Strum all six strings. Note that the first string [e] being open is what is creating the "6" in "G6". Make sure that you can hear that note when you strum this chord.

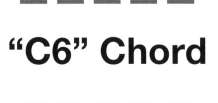

"C6" Chord

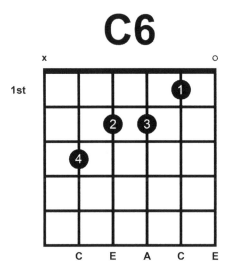

"C6" Chord Information:

- Number of Strings Used: Five (5)
- Level of Difficulty: Moderate
- Related Chords: Am, Em, G

Follow this fingering progression to play a "C6" chord:

Start by placing the index finger (1) on the first fret of the second string [B]. Then add your middle finger (2) to the second fret of the fourth string [D]. Next, add your ring finger (3) to the second fret of the third string [G]. Last, place your pinky finger (4) on the third fret of the fifth string [A]. All four fingers should make a tight package. With good up and down pressure and zero left to right slouching, all four fingers will fit in their proper places. Strum only the bottom five strings.

— — — — —

Six String Major Barre Chords

— — — — —

"F"

"F#" ("G♭")

"G#" ("A♭")

In this section you will learn six string major barre chords.

A note about barre chords

A barre chord is any chord that you play where at least one of your fingers on your fretting hand is holding down multiple strings. The advantage of barre chords is that they are moveable on the neck. In this section you will learn "F", "F#" ("G♭") and "G#" ("A♭"). Each of these barre chords is fretted the exact same, only on different locations on the fret board. For instance, an "F" chord begins on the first fret, whereas the "F#" ("G♭") begins on the second fret of the sixth string [E].

"F" Chord

F

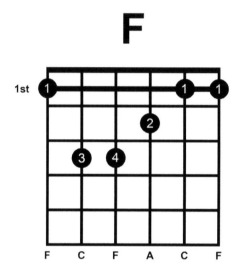

"F" Chord Information:

- Number of Strings Used: Six (6)
- Level of Difficulty: Hard
- Related Chords: C, Dm, G

Follow this fingering progression to play a "F" chord:

The first step is to lay your index finger (1) across all six strings on the first fret. You need to press down all the strings so that you can hear each note. Now that you have the first finger in place, add your ring (3) and pinky (4) fingers onto the third frets of the fifth [A] and fourth [D] strings, respectively. Last, add your middle finger (2) onto the second fret of the third [G] string. Once all in place, you should be able to strum across all six strings and produce an "F" chord. The first few times you strum you may have fret buzz or may not be able to produce sound at all. This chord takes practice. To rehearse this, take your hand off the guitar and then reposition it back to form a "F" chord.

"F#" ("G♭") Chord

F# (G♭)

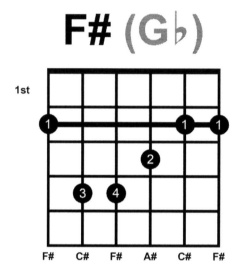

1st

F#   C#   F#   A#   C#   F#

"F#" ("G♭") Chord Information:

- Number of Strings Used: Six (6)
- Level of Difficulty: Hard
- Related Chords: B, C#, E

Follow this fingering progression to play a "F#" ("G♭") chord:

First, lay your index finger (1) across all six strings on the second fret. Next, add your ring (3) and pinky (4) fingers onto the fourth frets of the fifth [A] and fourth [D] strings, respectively. Finally, place your middle finger (2) onto the third fret of the third [G] string. Strum across all six strings. It is important that every string be heard in this chord. You may have a tendency to have some accidentally muted notes. Practice this chord to increase strength. Another name for "F#" is "G♭". They are one and the same. Please continue to note the alternate names of the #'s chords compared to ♭'s as you progress.

"G#" ("A♭") Chord

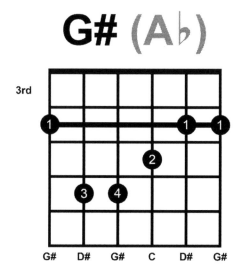

G# (A♭)

3rd

G#   D#   G#   C   D#   G#

"G#" ("A♭") Chord Information:

- Number of Strings Used: Six (6)
- Level of Difficulty: Hard
- Related Chords: C#, D#, F#

Follow this fingering progression to play a "G#" ("A♭") chord:

Begin by playing your pointer finger (1) across all six strings on the fourth fret. Then add your ring (3) and pinky (4) fingers on the sixth frets of the fifth [A] and fourth [D] strings. Last, place your middle finger (2) onto the fifth fret of the third [G] string. Strum all six strings. Practice this chord to increase strength. Another way to say "G#" is "A♭".

— — — — —

Five String Major Barre Chords

— — — — —

"A#" ("B♭")

"B"

"C#" ("D♭")

"D#" ("E♭")

In this section you will learn five string major barre chords.

A note about barre chords

A barre chord is any chord that you play where at least one of your fingers on your fretting hand is holding down multiple strings. The advantage of barre chords is that they are moveable on the neck. In this section you will learn "A#" ("B♭"), "B", "C#" ("D♭") and "D#" ("E♭"). Each of these barre chords is fretted the exact same, only on different locations of the fret board. For instance, a "A#" ("B♭") chord begins on the first fret, whereas the "B" begins on the second fret of the fifth string [A].

"A#" ("B♭") Chord

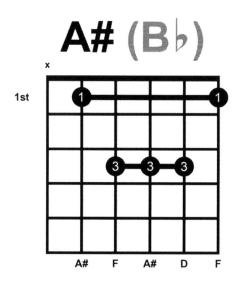

"A#" ("B♭") Chord Information:

- Number of Strings Used: Five (5)
- Level of Difficulty: Hard
- Related Chords: D#, F, G#

Follow this fingering progression to play an "A#" ("B♭") chord:

Begin by placing your pointer finger (1) as flat as you can across the first fret of the last five strings. Make sure to leave out the sixth string [E] for this chord. Last, add your ring finger (3) across the third fret of each of the fourth [D], third [G] and second [B] strings. Be careful to force your ring finger (3) to lay flat across all three strings. You cannot not mute the first [e] string that is currently being pressed down by your index finger (1). Strum the last five strings. This chord is difficult and will take time to practice. Do your best to come back to this chord each day until you have mastered it.

It is important to know that while "A#" and "B♭" are the same chord name, "B♭" is the commonly used name for this chord musically. Once more I stress, it is important that you know each of the # and ♭ chord names.

"B" Chord

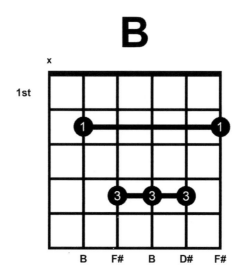

"B" Chord Information:
- Number of Strings Used: Five (5)
- Level of Difficulty: Hard
- Related Chords: E, F#, A

Follow this fingering progression to play a "B" chord:

Begin fingering the "B" by setting your index finger (1) on the second fret across the bottom five strings, omitting the sixth [E] string. Before we start the second barre, it is important that you have formed a strong hold, pressing firmly down on the second fret. Once in place, take your ring finger (3) and barre the fourth fret of the fourth [D], third [G], and second [B] strings. It is also important that you do not cover up the first string [e] that the index finger

(1) is currently pressing down on the second fret. You strum the last five strings, omitting the sixth string. Practice taking your fingers on and off the "B" shape.

"C#" ("D♭") Chord

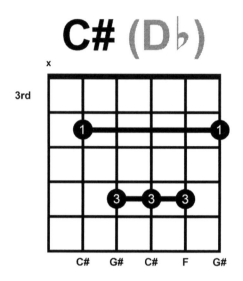

"C#" ("D♭") Chord Information:
- Number of Strings Used: Five (5)
- Level of Difficulty: Hard
- Related Chords: F#, G#, A#m

Follow this fingering progression to play a "C#" ("D♭") chord:

Start by taking your index finger (1) and lay it at as flat as you can across the fourth fret of all five strings, beginning at the fifth string [A] all the way across to the first string [e]. You can omit the sixth string [E] for this chord. The last addition is your ring finger (3) laid across the sixth fret of the fourth [D], third [G] and second [B] strings. As in other chords like this, making your ring finger (3) to lay flat across all three strings is difficult. You should not cover up the first [e] string that is currently being pressed down by your index finger (1). You can now strum the last five strings. Another name for "C#" is "D♭".

"D#" ("E♭") Chord

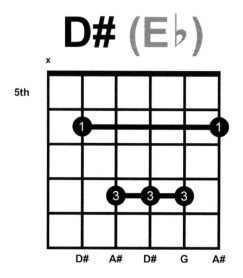

"D#" ("E♭") Chord Information:

- Number of Strings Used: Five (5)
- Level of Difficulty: Hard
- Related Chords: C#, A#, Cm

Follow this fingering progression to play a "D#" ("E♭") chord:

Begin fingering the "D#" ("E♭") by setting your index finger (1) on the sixth fret across the bottom five strings, omitting the sixth [E] string. Once in place, take your ring finger (3) and barre the eighth fret of the fourth [D], third [G], and second [B] strings. It is very important that you do not cover up the first string [e] that the index finger (1) is fretting the sixth fret. Only strum the last five strings, omitting the sixth string. It is also important to know that while "D#" and "E♭" are the same chord name, "E♭" is the commonly used name for this chord musically.

— — — — —

Six String Minor Barre Chords

— — — — —

"Fm"
"F#m" ("G♭m")
"Gm"
"G#m" ("A♭m")

In this section you will learn six string minor barre chords.

A note about barre chords

A barre chord is any chord that you play where at least one of your fingers on your fretting hand is holding down multiple strings. The advantage of barre chords is that they are moveable on the neck. In this section you will learn "Fm", "F#m" ("G♭m"), "Gm" and "G#m" ("A♭m"). Each of these barre chords is fretted the exact same, only on different locations on the fret board. For instance, an "Fm" chord begins on the first fret, whereas the "F#m" ("G♭m") begins on the second fret of the sixth string [E].

"Fm" Chord

Fm

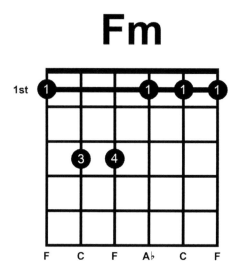

1st

F C F A♭ C F

"Fm" Chord Information:

- Number of Strings Used: Six (6)
- Level of Difficulty: Hard
- Related Chords: A♭, E♭, B♭

Follow this fingering progression to play a "Fm" chord:

The first step is to lay your index finger (1) across all six strings on the first fret. Next add your ring (3) and pinky (4) finger on the third frets of the fifth [A] and fourth [D] strings, respectively. Once each finger is in place, you should be able to strum across all six strings to produce a "Fm" chord. The difficult part of this chord is making sure to keep your barre on the first frets of the third [G], second [B] and first [e] strings. The minor note is the "A♭" created on the first fret of the third string [G]. Make sure you can hear that note.

"F#m" ("G♭m") Chord

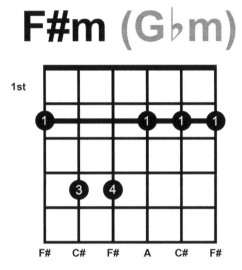

F#m (G♭m)

"F#m" ("G♭m") Chord Information:

- Number of Strings Used: Six (6)
- Level of Difficulty: Hard
- Related Chords: E, A, B

Follow this fingering progression to play a "F#m" ("G♭m") chord:

The first step is to lay your index finger (1) across all six strings on the second fret. Next add your ring (3) and pinky (4) fingers on the fourth frets of the fifth [A] and fourth [D] strings, respectively. Once in place, you should be able to strum across all six strings and produce an "F#m" ("G♭m") chord. Be careful to make sure you hear all six strings completely. It is important that you hear the second fret note on the third [G] string as that is what is making the chord a minor. The other way to say "F#m" is "G♭m".

"Gm" Chord

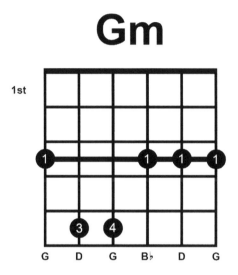

"Gm" Chord Information:
- Number of Strings Used: Six (6)
- Level of Difficulty: Hard
- Related Chords: B♭, F, E♭

Follow this fingering progression to play a "Gm" chord:

First, lay your index finger (1) across all six strings on the third fret. Then add your ring (3) and pinky (4) finger to the fifth frets of the fifth [A] and fourth [D] strings, respectively. Once in place, you should be able to strum across all six strings to produce a "Gm" chord. It is important that you hear the third fret note on the third [G] string. As in the other six string minor chords, that third fret note is what is making the "Gm" a minor chord.

"G#m" ("A♭m") Chord

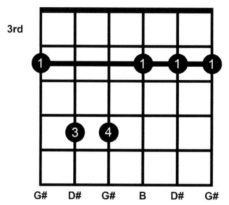

G# D# G# B D# G#

"G#m" ("A♭m") Chord Information:

- Number of Strings Used: Six (6)
- Level of Difficulty: Hard
- Related Chords: B, E, F#

Follow this fingering progression to play a "G#m" ("A♭m") chord:

To begin, lay your pointer finger (1) across all six strings on the fourth fret. Next, add your ring (3) and pinky (4) fingers to the sixth frets of the fifth [A] and fourth [D] strings, respectively. Strum all six strings. It is important to make sure that the fourth string [D] can be heard while pressing down the fourth fret with your index finger (1). That note is the *minor* note of the "G#m" ("A♭m") chord. The other name for "G#m" is "A♭m".

Five String Minor Barre Chords

"A#m" ("B♭m")
"Bm"
"Cm"
"C#m" ("D♭m")
"D#m" ("E♭m")

In this section you will learn five string minor barre chords.

A note about barre chords

A barre chord is any chord that you play where at least one of your fingers on your fretting hand is holding down multiple strings. The advantage of barre chords is that they are moveable on the neck. In this section you will learn "A#m" ("B♭m"), "Bm", "Cm", "C#m" ("D♭m") and "D#m" ("E♭m"). Each of these barre chords is fretted the exact same, only on different locations on the fret board. For instance, a "A#m" ("B♭m") chord begins on the first fret, whereas the "Bm" begins on the second fret of the fifth string [A].

"A#m" ("B♭m") Chord

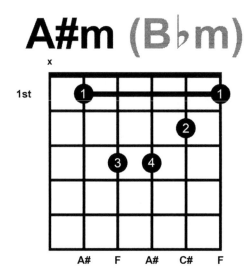

"A#m" ("B♭m") Chord Information:

- Number of Strings Used: Five (5)
- Level of Difficulty: Hard
- Related Chords: C#, G#, F#

Follow this fingering progression to play an "A#m" ("B♭m") chord:

Start by taking your index finger (1) and lay it across the first fret of all five strings, beginning at the fifth string [A] all the way across to the first string [e]. You should omit the sixth string [E]. Next add your middle finger (2) onto the second fret of the second string [B]. Be sure that your first fret barre has not lost its strength. Last, add your ring finger (3) and your pinky finger (4) to the third frets of the fourth [D] and third [G] strings, respectively. Once all fingers are in place, only strum the last five strings, leaving out the sixth string [E] that is not being pressed down. The other way to say "A#m" is "B♭m".

"Bm" Chord

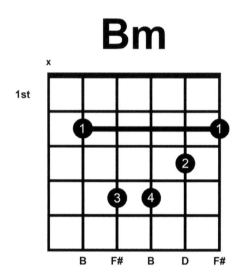

"Bm" Chord Information:
- Number of Strings Used: Five (5)
- Level of Difficulty: Hard
- Related Chords: A, E, D

Follow this fingering progression to play a "Bm" chord:

Begin by placing your index finger (1) as flat as you can across the second fret of all five strings beginning at the fifth string [A] on to the first string [e]. You can omit the sixth string [E] for this chord. The first additional finger to add is your middle finger (2) onto the third fret of the second string [B]. Confirm that your barre has not lost it's strength. Last, add your ring finger (3) and your pinky finger (4) to the fourth frets of the fourth [D] and third [G] strings, respectively. Once all fingers are in place you will strum the last five strings, leaving out the sixth string [E]. Take your hand off the guitar and begin the sequence of fretting again.

"Cm" Chord

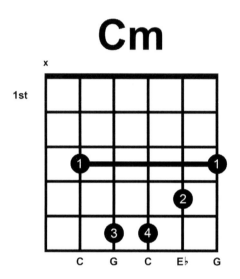

"Cm" Chord Information:

- Number of Strings Used: Five (5)
- Level of Difficulty: Hard
- Related Chords: E♭, A♭, B♭

Follow this fingering progression to play a "Cm" chord:

Start by taking your index finger (1) and lay it at as flat as you can across the third fret of all five strings beginning at the fifth string [A] all to the way to the first string [e]. Omit the sixth string [E] for this chord. Next, add your middle finger (2) onto the fourth fret of the second string [B]. Confirm that your barre has not lost it's strength. Last, add your ring finger (3) and your pinky finger (4) to the fifth frets of the fourth [D] and third [G] strings, respectively. Once all fingers are in place you will strum the last five strings, leaving out the sixth string [E] that is not being pressed down.

"C#m" ("D♭m") Chord

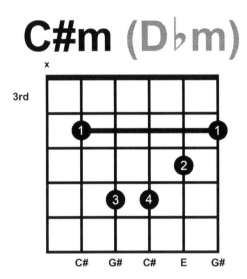

C#m (D♭m)

"C#m" ("D♭m") Chord Information:

- Number of Strings Used: Five (5)
- Level of Difficulty: Hard
- Related Chords: B, E, A

Follow this fingering progression to play a "C#m" ("D♭m") chord:

Begin by laying your index finger (1) as flat as you can across the fourth fret of all five strings, beginning at the fifth string [A] all the way across to the first string [e]. As in the preceding chords, you should omit the sixth string [E] for this chord. The next finger to add is your middle finger (2) onto the fifth fret of the second string [B]. Remember to be sure that your barre has not lost its strength. Last, add your ring finger (3) and your pinky finger (4) to the sixth frets of the fourth [D] and third [G] strings, respectively. Once all fingers are in place, you will only strum the last five strings, leaving out the sixth string [E] that is not being pressed down. Take your hand off the guitar and begin the sequence of fretting again. As with your other chords, you will need to practice this chord often. "C#m" and "D♭m" are one and the same name.

"D#m" ("E♭m") Chord

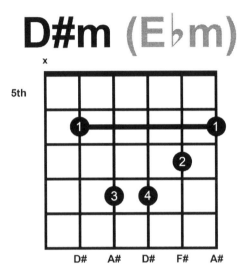

"D#m" ("E♭m") Chord Information:

- Number of Strings Used: Five (5)
- Level of Difficulty: Hard
- Related Chords: C#, F#, B

Follow this fingering progression to play a "D#m" ("E♭m") chord:

First, begin by placing your index finger (1) as flat as you are able across the sixth fret of all five strings, beginning at the fifth string [A] across to the first string [e]. You should leave out the sixth string [E] for this chord. The next finger to add is your middle finger (2) onto the seventh fret of the second string [B]. Last, add your ring finger (3) and your pinky finger (4) to the eighth frets of the fourth [D] and third [G] strings, respectively. Once all fingers are in place, you will only strum the last five strings, leaving out the sixth string [E] that is not being pressed down. The other way to say "D#m" is "E♭m".

- - - - -

Final Greetings

You've done it! 42 guitar chords are now under your belt! Quick, play a "C#"! HA! Now that you know so many more chords, it is time to put them to use. If you are not involved in your local church in their music ministry somehow, why not? You have an entire tool box of chords and knowledge that may be helpful to them. If you are on a worship team, it is time to implement what you've learned. Use some of your new barre chords rather than transcribing your sheet music for capo use. You are ready!

Blessing!

"I pray that with each of these chords you have learned you will be used mightily for the kingdom of God. May the LORD honor your investment in his kingdom as you go forward worshiping him. I pray that God will lead you in all that you do and open wide the gates of heaven to you! In Jesus' name, amen."

Appendix

How to buy a guitar. A quick and easy guide of the things you have to know before you head to a guitar store!

"Friends never let friends go into a guitar store alone."

Here's how to buy a guitar! IMPORTANT: Never go into a guitar store to buy a guitar without facts about the price and availability of that guitar in your area. Most music store salesmen are about as motivated as used car salesmen. They know which guitars have the highest margin. If you go into your store without a plan you may come out with your salesman's favorite pick, but what may not be the best guitar for you in the long run. My recommendation is that you take an experienced guitar player whom you trust with you.

A note about price range.

I am often asked "What guitar should I get?". My answer is always the same: "What's your price range?". Acoustic guitars in particular live in specific price bands. The entry level acoustic usually ranges: $100-$300. The intermediate: $500-$1,000. And the professional: $1,000 and up. I intentionally left out the $300-$500 range. The biggest difference between an entry level and an intermediate guitar is the type of wood and binding that the luthier, or guitar maker, uses to create the instrument. You will discover better instruments as you cross the $500 barrier. Normally you will not notice a significant difference between a guitar for $250 and one for $400. I recommend beginner guitarists purchase in the $250-$300 range. You may find an acoustic guitar for $299 and then the same guitar for $449, but with electronics (making it an acoustic electric guitar). Don't be fooled into paying that extra $150 for electronics that cost the manufacturer $8 to install. The majority of their cost is in drilling the holes in the wood. Rather, buy the nicest $299 acoustic guitar you can find and then add the electronics later. You will be glad you did. The sound quality when plugged in will be much better. When you begin to look at intermediate or professional guitars is the instance when you may want to consider an onboard pickup and electronics package that comes pre-installed. Most of the time those pickups are hand selected for that particular instrument and are a part of the guitar's original design.

Ask for a bundle.

While you are negotiating the final price for your guitar, consider asking for a few items as part of a bundle. You will want a new set of strings. You don't know how long your guitar has been on the shelf, being played by possibly hundreds of people. You will also need a strap (get one you like), a tuner (if you have a smart phone you could download an app) and you will want to buy a capo.

Spring for the case.

Finally, spring for the hardshell case that is made for your guitar. Unlike a grand piano that moves once a decade, your guitar is small enough to go places. It will be in your trunk with all your baseball gear. Maybe your little sister will have to sit on it in the middle row of your parent's minivan. Who knows? Get the case that fits your guitar snugly so that it is best protected when you are not performing or practicing.

Go in with a plan. Do your homework!

To sum up, go to your music store with a plan (and with a musician friend) and be prepared to negotiate for a bundled price. Also, remember to budget for a hardshell case if you are able. Some stores may want to sell you a warranty. While I am sure it seems tempting, typically warranties have deductibles and are not worth all they are said to be worth. Since you may be buying a lower end instrument (especially if this is your first), know that you are going to get scratches, bumps and bruises on it. In my opinion, you may want to disregard the store's warranty pitch. That's it! Happy buying!

Chord Families Diagram

The diagram below will help you know what chords belong in which chord family. For instance, in the key of "G", the "G" chord is the most important with the "C" and "D" chords being secondarily important. In the key of "D" the "D" is most important while the "G" and "A" are secondary. Use this diagram to become more familiar with keys and chord families.

Chord Families

Key	1	2m	3m	4	5	6m	7dim
G	G	Am	Bm	C	D	Em	F#dim
G# (Ab)	G# (Ab)	A#m (Bbm)	Cm	C# (Db)	D# (Eb)	Fm	Gdim
A	A	Bm	C#m	D	E	F#m	G#dim
A# (Bb)	A# (Bb)	Cm	Dm	D# (Eb)	F	Gm	Adim
B	B	C#m	D#m	E	F#	G#m	A#dim
C	C	Dm	Em	F	G	Am	Bdim
C# (Db)	C# (Db)	D#m (Ebm)	Fm	F# (Gb)	G# (Ab)	A#m (Bbm)	Cdim
D	D	Em	F#m	G	A	Bm	C#dim
D# (Eb)	D# (Eb)	Fm	Gm	G# (Ab)	A# (Bb)	Cm	Ddim
E	E	F#m	G#m	A	B	C#m	D#dim
F	F	Gm	Am	Bb	C	Dm	Edim
F# (Gb)	F# (Gb)	G#m (Abm)	A#m (Bbm)	B	C# (Db)	D#m (Ebm)	Fdim

About The Author

Micah Brooks is a worship pastor, author and songwriter from Nashville, Tennessee, USA. His passion is to see Jesus' people lift up and worship Jesus' name.

While playing music is part of his profession, Micah is a family man in life. He is married to wife Rochelle. Together they have three children (as of 2016, they may have more now ha!): Liam, Aisley and Jovie. They attend World Outreach Church where Micah is a worship pastor. The whole family enjoys running in the Tennessee heat and Micah enjoys playing church league softball.

Micah has been a guitar teacher and coach for over ten years. Most people learn best by having one-on-one instruction. This book and the others in this series, such as *Worship Guitar In Six Weeks*, were created with the student in mind. They are each the best of the lessons that a guitar student will receive from Micah. The guitar is one of the greatest tools we have for modern worship. When the guitar is used to expand God's kingdom, the opportunities are endless. All glory to Jesus Christ!

You can find out more about Micah Brooks including his other books, music, videos, websites and resources at www.micahbrooks.com.

Additional Resources

Find out about the other books in this series and sign up for the Micah Brooks "Stay Connected" mailing list.

This is book two in the Micah Brooks Guitar Authority Series books. *Worship Guitar In Six Weeks* is a six week course designed to bring a guitar player from knowing little about guitar onto the stage in six weeks. Please pass it along to your friends! Also, the next book in this series is called *Guitar Secrets Revealed*. Learn what the guitar professionals know without needing to spend years to acquire that information. Find out about the Micah Brooks Guitar Authority Series books and more at:

www.micahbrooks.com

Email Micah

Email Micah Brooks at micah@micahbrooks.com. I want to know who you are. I have a heart to meet people. It is my privilege to respond to my emails personally. Please feel free to connect with me. I will glad to answer questions or set up a Skype call as you need.

Join the Micah Brooks "Stay Connected" mailing list to stay up to date

Subscribe to the Micah Brooks Ministry "Stay Connected" mailing list and stay current with my latest book releases. My email list is always free and intended to deliver high value content to your inbox. I do not sell your email address to anyone else. I simply want to be able to stay connected with you. Click here to join my mailing list.

www.micahbrooks.com/join

Reviews on Amazon

Reviews are the lifeblood of authors. If you are willing to leave feedback, I would be humbled and grateful. Please do so at:

www.amazon.com

Skype Lessons

I would be glad to consider giving you online guitar lessons. If you would like to apply for lessons with Micah Brooks via Skype visit my website to find out more. I cannot accept every student, but I would be happy to hear your story and see what you would like to accomplish.

www.micahbrooks.com

Join The Christian Guitar Community Facebook Group

All readers of this book are welcome to join The Christian Guitar Community Facebook group. Meet guitar players from around the world. You may post your insights about learning guitar. You are welcome to ask questions and comment on other posts. The group is designed to be a community. We ask everyone in the group to interact, which makes the content fun and engaging.

www.facebook.com/groups/thechristianguitarcommunity

More About Micah Brooks Ministry

For more about Micah Brooks and my ministry, including books, CDs, mp3s, clothing and art designs, online store, blogs, devotions, speaking and performing dates please go to:

www.micahbrooks.com

Follow Micah Brooks

Everyone is welcome to follow Micah Brooks on these social media platforms:

Facebook: @micahbrookspage
www.facebook.com/micahbrookspage

Twitter: @mchbrks
www.twitter.com/mchbrks

LinkedIn: Micah Brooks
www.linkedin.com/in/micahbrooks

Instagram: @mchbrks
www.instagram.com/mchbrks

If you have trouble connecting to any of these social media accounts, please visit www.micahbrooks.com.

Micah is Editor In Chief at www.worshippublishing.com, www.uprightpassiveincome.com and www.songwritingcreative.com

Worship Publishing is a resource website that includes books, daily devotions, music, podcasts, product reviews and many more recommendations. Use our wealth of staff writers and high quality guest post content to better your walk with the Lord. Visit: www.worshippublishing.com

Upright Passive Income is a company devoted to helping entrepreneurs achieve their vision and dreams. Everyone should have a side business of some kind and earning passive income is an awesome way to do so. Great examples include self-publishing a book, affiliate marketing and video marketing. Visit: www.uprightpassiveincome.com to learn about all of our high quality services.

Songwriting Creative is a website devoted to songwriting in all forms. From beginner writers to the most advanced, we each still have room to grow and expand our skills and craft. www.songwritingcreative.com is intended to be a songwriting community and we do our best to facilitate. Check it out.

Made in the USA
Middletown, DE
08 February 2017